pancakes
and waffles

Kate Habershon

pancakes

and waffles

photography by William Lingwood

RYLAND
PETERS
& SMALL

LONDON NEW YORK

Designer Catherine Randy
Commissioning Editor Elsa Petersen-Schepelern
Editor Jennifer Herman
Production Patricia Harrington
Art Director Gabriella Le Grazie
Publishing Director Alison Starling

Food Stylist Kate Habershon
Cooking Assistant Becca Hetherston
Stylist Antonia Gaunt
Photographer's Assistant Emma Bentham-Wood

First published in USA in 2002
by Ryland Peters & Small, Inc.
519 Broadway, 5th Floor
New York, NY 10012
www.rylandpeters.com
10 9 8 7 6 5 4 3 2 1

Hardback ISBN: 1 84172 343 6
Paperback ISBN: 1 84172 382 7

Library of Congress Cataloging-in-Publication Data
Habershon, Kate.
  Pancakes & waffles / Kate Habershon;
  photography by William Lingwood.
     p. cm.
  Includes index.
  ISBN 1-84172-343-6
   1. Pancakes, waffles, etc. I. Title.
TX770.P34 H33 2002
641.8'15--dc21   2002066758

Printed in China

Notes
All spoon measurements are level
unless otherwise indicated. Batters
for pancakes and waffles vary in
consistency, which in turn affects
the accuracy of tablespoon
measurements. In this book,
tablespoon measures for mixed
batters should be taken as heaped,
rather than level.

The number of pancakes cooked in
each batch will depend on the size
of the skillet used.

Waffle irons and waffle makers vary
in size. Most take about ½ cup of
batter. Spoon in just enough mixture
so that it almost covers the base,
leaving enough room for the waffle
to spread. Alternatively, follow the
manufacturer's instructions.

All eggs are large, unless otherwise
specified. Uncooked or partly cooked
eggs should not be served to the
very young, the very old, those with
compromised immune systems, or
pregnant women.

contents

For a beautiful breakfast ...

The all-American breakfast, what image does that conjure? For me, it's pancakes and waffles piled high and loaded with butter, warm maple syrup, and slices of crisp bacon. They appear on just about every breakfast menu, and the choices are endless and often highly creative. I love the way even the most modest diners offer their own unique variations—blueberry, ginger, pumpkin, and potato. As for the toppings, they are too numerous to list.

The word 'waffle' is derived from the old French word for 'honeycomb' and referred to the distinctive pattern made by the waffle iron. The style varied from region to region in France, from light and crisp, to heavy and buttery. But it is the Belgian version which is probably the most popular these days: with its crisp crust and silky interior, it is waffle perfection, and has found its way to all corners of the world.

In Europe, waffles and pancakes are associated less with home cooking and more with street food; a hot treat on a cold day out. It's common to find street vendors selling hot, sugar-dredged waffles, smothered in jam and cream. If you follow your nose, you'll find the nearest crêperie—the heavenly aroma of melted chocolate and spiced apples is hard to ignore.

While still strongly associated with breakfast, clearly waffles and pancakes are no longer confined to the breakfast table. With such a wide choice of toppings and consistencies, these simple batters can form the basis of a delicious meal or a wonderful snack at any time of the day—enjoy! I have had enormous fun putting this book together—I do hope you have as much enjoyment adding these recipes to your repertoire.

perfect pancakes

Everyone has a favorite pancake recipe and this is mine—well risen with a soft texture ready to soak up syrup like a sponge. Serve with your choice of syrups, fruit, cream, or butter.

Simple Pancake Stack

1½ cups
all-purpose flour

2½ teaspoons
baking powder

1 teaspoon salt

3 tablespoons sugar

1 cup milk

3 eggs

4 tablespoons
unsalted butter,
melted and cooled

To serve (optional)

maple syrup or other
sauces (pages 60–63)

unsalted butter or
whipped butter
(page 16)

*a flat griddle pan or
skillet, preheated and
lightly greased*

Serves 4

Makes 8 medium
or 4 large pancakes

Sift the flour, baking powder, salt, and sugar into a bowl. Put the milk, eggs, and cooled melted butter into a second large bowl, then mix with a wire whisk. Add the sifted dry ingredients and beat gently to make a thick batter. Be careful not to overwork the mixture—it doesn't matter if the batter isn't smooth.

Heat the prepared griddle or skillet over medium heat. Reduce the heat. Pour about 3 tablespoons of batter into the skillet and cook in batches of 3–4 for 1 minute over low heat until small bubbles begin to appear on the surface and the underside is golden brown. Turn the pancake over and cook the other side for 1 minute. Transfer to a plate and keep warm in a low oven while you cook the remainder—use 3 tablespoons of batter for each pancake.

Serve immediately with maple syrup and butter.

The all-American classic, loved by millions. Use fresh or frozen berries, but I prefer frozen because they take slightly longer to cook and don't burn so quickly.

Blueberry Sour Cream Pancakes
with Maple Syrup Pecans

1½ cups all-purpose flour

2 teaspoons baking powder

1 teaspoon salt

¼ cup sugar

2 eggs, separated

1 cup sour cream

⅔ cup milk

4 tablespoons unsalted butter, melted and cooled

8 oz. blueberries, fresh or frozen

vanilla ice cream, to serve

Maple syrup pecans

4 oz. pecans

1 cup maple syrup

4 tablespoons unsalted butter

a baking tray

a flat griddle pan or skillet, preheated and lightly greased

Serves 4
Makes 8–10 pancakes

To make the maple syrup pecans, spread the nuts over a baking tray and cook in a preheated oven at 400°F for 5 minutes until lightly toasted. Heat the maple syrup in a small saucepan and simmer gently for 3 minutes. Remove from the heat and stir in the pecans and butter.

To make the pancakes, sift the flour, baking powder, salt, and sugar into a bowl. Put the egg yolks, sour cream, milk, and cooled melted butter into a second bowl and beat well, then add the flour mixture all at once and beat until smooth. Put the egg whites into a clean bowl and beat until soft peaks form. Fold them gently into the batter, then fold in the blueberries. Don't overmix— a few lumps of flour and egg white don't matter.

Heat the prepared griddle or skillet over medium heat. Reduce the heat. Pour about 3 tablespoons of batter into the pan and cook in batches of 3–4 for 1–2 minutes over very low heat to avoid burning the blueberries, until small bubbles begin to appear on the surface and the underside is golden brown. Turn them over and cook the other side for 1 minute. Transfer to a plate and keep them warm in a low oven while you cook the remainder.

Serve with ice cream and the maple syrup pecans.

Gingerbread Pancakes

Ground ginger and molasses are the key to any gingerbread recipe. Grated fresh ginger or chopped crystallized ginger can be used to add a little texture.

1½ cups all-purpose flour

2 teaspoons baking powder

½ teaspoon baking soda

½ teaspoon salt

2 teaspoons ground ginger

2 teaspoons ground cinnamon

1 teaspoon ground cloves

2 eggs

¼ cup firmly packed brown sugar

1 cup buttermilk

2 tablespoons molasses

4 tablespoons unsalted butter, melted and cooled

To serve
warm apple marmalade (page 62)
cool sour cream

a flat griddle pan or skillet, preheated and lightly greased

Serves 4
Makes 12 pancakes

Sift the flour, baking powder, baking soda, salt, ginger, cinnamon, and cloves into a bowl. Put the eggs and brown sugar into a second bowl and beat well with a wire whisk. Beat in the buttermilk, molasses, cooled melted butter, and ½ cup water. Add the flour mixture and beat once or twice until almost smooth. Don't overwork the mixture—remember lumps are good.

Heat the prepared griddle or skillet over medium heat. Reduce the heat. Pour about 2 tablespoons of batter into the pan, spread with the back of a spoon, and cook in batches of 3–4 for 1 minute over low heat, until small bubbles begin to appear on the surface and the underside is golden brown. Turn them over and cook the other side for 1 minute. Transfer to a plate and keep them warm in a low oven while you cook the remainder.

Serve with apple marmalade and sour cream.

Triple Chocolate Pancakes

Complete chocolate overload! Packed with velvety melted chocolate and finished with sweet and sour taste of smooth white chocolate yogurt. Adults only.

1½ cups all-purpose flour

¾ cup unsweetened cocoa powder

1 teaspoon baking powder

1 teaspoon baking soda

¼ cup sugar

¾ cup milk

½ cup buttermilk

2 eggs, separated

3 tablespoons unsalted butter, melted and cooled

½ teaspoon salt

3 oz. bittersweet chocolate, chopped

3 oz. white chocolate, chopped

hot chocolate sauce (page 60), to serve

White chocolate yogurt

6 oz. white chocolate

¼ cup plain yogurt

blini pans (5 inches diameter), a flat griddle pan, or skillet, preheated and lightly greased

Serves 4–6

Makes 12 pancakes

Sift the flour, cocoa, baking powder, baking soda, and sugar into a bowl. Put the milk, buttermilk, egg yolks, and cooled melted butter into a second large bowl and beat well. Add the flour mixture and mix thoroughly.

Put the egg whites and salt into a clean bowl and beat with a wire whisk until stiff peaks form. Add 1 tablespoon of the egg whites to the chocolate mixture and stir to loosen it, then carefully fold in the remaining egg whites, then the bittersweet and white chocolate.

Heat the prepared blini pans, griddle, or skillet over medium heat. Reduce the heat. Pour about 2 tablespoons of batter into the pan and cook in batches of 3–4 over low heat for about 1 minute, or until small bubbles begin to appear on the surface and the underside is golden brown. Turn the pancakes over and cook the other side for 1 minute. Transfer to a plate and keep them warm in a low oven while you cook the remainder.

To make white chocolate yogurt, put the chocolate into a bowl set over a saucepan of simmering water and melt slowly. Remove from the heat and let cool a little, then beat in the yogurt until smooth and shiny. Serve with the pancakes and hot chocolate sauce.

Silver Dollar Pancakes

Although these mini-pancakes are a children's favorite, many adults harbor a secret passion for them as well.

1 cup all-purpose flour

1½ teaspoons baking powder

2 tablespoons sugar

½ teaspoon salt

2 eggs, separated

¾ cup milk

unsalted butter, for frying

blueberry sauce (page 62), to serve

Whipped butter (optional)

2 sticks unsalted butter, softened

2 tablespoons milk

a flat griddle pan or skillet, preheated and lightly greased

Serves 4–6

Makes 40 small pancakes

Sift the flour, baking powder, sugar, and salt into a bowl. Put the egg yolks and milk into another bowl and gently beat in the sifted dry ingredients. Put the egg whites into a clean bowl and beat with a wire whisk until stiff peaks form. Using a metal spoon, fold them into the batter.

Heat the prepared griddle or skillet over medium heat. Reduce the heat. Pour 1 teaspoon of batter into the pan and cook in batches of 6–8 for 2 minutes over low heat, until small bubbles begin to appear on the surface and the underside is golden brown. Turn the pancakes over and cook the other side for 1 minute. Transfer to a plate and keep them warm in a low oven while you cook the remainder, brushing the pan with butter as necessary.

Meanwhile, to make the whipped butter, put the butter and milk into a small bowl and beat until pale and light.

Serve the pancakes with whipped butter and blueberry sauce, or your choice of other accompaniments.

These pretty speckled pancakes are a treat. Orange zest gives the recipe a fresh edge while the poppy seeds provide a little crunch. Beware of the honey—too much and the pancakes will brown too quickly without giving the center enough time to cook.

Poppyseed Pancakes
with Spiced Clementines

1 cup all-purpose flour

½ teaspoon baking powder

½ teaspoon baking soda

2½ tablespoons firmly packed brown sugar

⅓ cup poppyseeds

1 egg

1 tablespoon honey

⅓ cup sour cream

⅓ cup milk

8 oz. mascarpone cheese, to serve

Spiced clementines

4 clementines or small oranges

¼ cup spiced brown sugar (page 61)

a flat griddle or skillet, preheated and lightly greased

Serves 4
Makes 10–12 small pancakes

To make the spiced clementines, grate the zest of 2 of the fruit for use in the pancakes, then peel all 4, removing as much of the bitter white pith as possible. Using a sharp knife, finely slice the fruit crosswise. Arrange the fruit on a plate, sprinkle with the spiced sugar, and set aside to infuse.

To make the pancakes, sift the flour, baking powder, and baking soda into a large bowl, then stir in the brown sugar and poppyseeds.

Put the egg, honey, sour cream, and milk into a second large bowl, then add the reserved grated zest of the clementines. Beat well, then add the flour mixture all at once and keep beating until just smooth.

Heat the prepared griddle or skillet over medium heat. Reduce the heat. Pour 1 tablespoon of batter into the pan and cook in batches of 3–4 for 1 minute over low heat, until small bubbles begin to appear on the surface and the underside is golden brown. Turn them over and cook the other side for 1 minute. Transfer to a plate and keep them warm in a low oven while you cook the remainder.

To serve, layer the poppyseed pancakes with slices of clementines and spoonfuls of mascarpone.

Overnight Pancakes
with Tropical Fruit and Mango and Ginger Purée

2 cups all-purpose flour

2 tablespoons sugar or vanilla sugar

1 teaspoon active dry yeast

1 teaspoon salt

1½ cups milk

7 tablespoons unsalted butter, melted and cooled, plus extra for frying

2 eggs

To serve

assorted tropical fruit, such as mango, starfruit (carambola), kiwifruit, passionfruit, and papaya

mango and ginger purée (page 63)

2 tablespoons sesame seeds, pan-toasted in a dry skillet

a flat griddle pan or skillet, preheated and lightly greased

Serves 4–6
Makes 10–12 pancakes

I love yeasted recipes because it means all the hard work is done the night before, so breakfast is a breeze. Mango and ginger purée takes seconds to prepare. I like to do this recipe when I have a house full of people—it's perfect for a summer morning.

Sift the flour, sugar, yeast, and salt into a large bowl, then carefully mix in the milk and melted butter to make a thick batter. Cover the bowl and leave at room temperature overnight.

Next morning, separate the eggs and stir the yolks into the batter. Put the egg whites into a clean bowl, beat with a wire whisk until stiff peaks form, then gently fold them in with a metal spoon.

Heat the prepared griddle or skillet over medium heat. Reduce the heat. Pour about 2–3 tablespoons of batter into the pan and cook in batches of 3–4 for 1 minute over low heat, until small bubbles begin to appear on the surface and the underside is golden brown. Turn the pancakes over and cook the other side for about 2 minutes. Transfer to a plate and keep them warm in a low oven while you cook the remainder.

Serve immediately with fresh fruit and a spoonful of mango and ginger purée, sprinkled with pan-toasted sesame seeds.

1 cup all-purpose flour

⅓ cup ground rice or semolina

3 tablespoons firmly packed brown sugar

½ teaspoon freshly grated nutmeg

1 tablespoon baking powder

½ teaspoon salt

1 egg

½ cup milk

½ cup plain yogurt

4 small ripe bananas, 2 mashed, 2 sliced

unsalted butter, for frying

Toffee walnut sauce

1 tablespoons unsalted butter

3 oz. walnuts, coarsely chopped

1 recipe toffee sauce (page 61)

a flat griddle pan or skillet, preheated and lightly greased

Serves 4

Makes 8 small or 4 large pancakes

Sift the flour, ground rice, sugar, nutmeg, baking powder, and salt into a large bowl. Put the egg, milk, and yogurt into another bowl, beat well, then add the 2 mashed bananas. Beat the flour mixture into the egg mixture—don't be tempted to beat it smooth!

Heat the prepared griddle or skillet over medium heat. Reduce the heat. Pour 2 tablespoons of batter into the pan and press 3 slices of banana onto the pancake. Cook in batches of 3–4 for about 1 minute over low heat, or until small bubbles begin to appear on the surface and the underside is golden brown. Turn the pancakes over and cook the other side for about 2–3 minutes. They are about 4 inches diameter—cook as many as your pan will hold at once and keep them warm on a plate in a low oven while you cook the remainder. To make large pancakes, use ¼ cup each.

Meanwhile, to make the toffee walnut sauce, melt the butter in a large skillet, add the nuts, and stir over high heat until they smell toasted and are lightly browned. Drain on paper towels. Warm the toffee sauce in a saucepan over low heat and stir in the nuts.

Serve the pancakes, banana side up, with toffee walnut sauce.

Banana Pancakes
with Toffee Walnut Sauce

Whenever Americans find themselves in the wilder parts of the world and they start to pine for familiar food, it's apple pie and banana pancakes that remind them of home. These pancakes are a dressed-up version, glamorous enough for a special brunch party—or just for a weekend breakfast for the family.

Add sliced fruit to the top of any pancake to turn it into something special. Some fruits burn more quickly than others, so take care.

Date and Pistachio Griddle Cakes

1⅓ cups all-purpose flour

2 teaspoons baking powder

1 teaspoon salt

3 tablespoons firmly packed brown sugar

⅔ cup rolled oats

4 oz. shelled, unsalted pistachios, coarsely chopped

4 oz. pitted dates, finely chopped

1 cup milk

2 eggs

4 tablespoons unsalted butter, melted and cooled, plus extra for brushing

grated zest of 1 lemon

2 apples

To serve

fresh honeycomb (optional)

plain yogurt or sour cream

a star-shaped cookie cutter

a flat griddle pan or skillet, preheated and lightly greased

Serves 4
Makes 12 griddle cakes

Sift the flour, baking powder, and salt into a large bowl, then stir in the sugar, oats, nuts, and dates. Put the milk, eggs, cooled melted butter, and lemon zest into another bowl, beat well, then add the nut and oat mixture and stir gently. (Be careful not to overwork the mixture—it doesn't matter if the dough isn't smooth.)

Before you begin to cook the griddle cakes, prepare the apple by slicing it horizontally into ⅛-inch rings and removing the core of each slice with a cookie cutter (a star shape works best).

Heat the prepared griddle or skillet over medium heat. Reduce the heat. Pour 1 tablespoon of batter onto the griddle and top with an apple slice. Cook in batches of 3–4 for 2–3 minutes over low heat, or until small bubbles begin to appear on the surface and the underside is golden brown. Brush the apple slice with a little melted butter, then turn the pancakes over and cook the other side for about 2 minutes. Repeat until all the mixture and apple slices have been used. Transfer to a plate and keep them warm in a low oven while you cook the remainder.

Serve with honeycomb, if using, and yogurt.

2 cups pine nuts

½ cup all-purpose flour

2 teaspoons baking powder

½ teaspoon salt

¾ cup instant polenta

2 tablespoons sugar

½ cup milk

2 eggs

2 tablespoons unsalted butter, melted and cooled

grated zest of 1 orange

To serve

confectioners' sugar

orange and cardamom syrup (page 62)

a flat griddle pan or large skillet, preheated and lightly greased

Makes 40 pancakes

Put the pine nuts into a dry skillet and cook over a low heat, stirring constantly, until just brown. Transfer to a plate and let cool.

Sift the flour, baking powder, and salt into a bowl and stir in the polenta and sugar.

Put the milk, eggs, cooled melted butter, and orange zest into a bowl, beat well, then add the polenta mixture and beat until smooth. Stir in 1½ cups of the pine nuts and let the mixture stand for 5 minutes to soften the polenta and thicken the batter.

Heat the prepared griddle or skillet over medium heat. Reduce the heat. Pour 1 tablespoon of batter onto the pan and sprinkle with a few of the remaining pine nuts. Cook in batches of 6–8 for about 2 minutes over low heat, or until small bubbles begin to appear on the surface and the underside is golden brown. Turn the pancakes over and cook the other side for about 2 minutes. Transfer to a plate and keep them warm in a low oven while you cook the remainder.

Serve sprinkled with sifted confectioners' sugar, with the syrup poured over or served separately.

Pine Nut and Polenta Pennycakes

Bite-size, nutty pancakes dredged in confectioners' sugar are perfect to finish off a supper with friends. Serve the pennycakes with a huge bowl of cardamom syrup for communal dipping.

Cornmeal and Bacon Breakfast Stack

Masa harina and chile give this recipe a slightly Mexican flavor. Try these pancakes with huevos rancheros or even avocado salsa.

²/₃ cup all-purpose flour

1½ teaspoons baking powder

1 teaspoon salt

½ cup masa harina or fine yellow cornmeal

1 egg, separated

½ cup buttermilk

¾ cup milk

2 tablespoons freshly grated Parmesan cheese

6 oz. prosciutto or bacon, coarsely chopped

4 scallions, cut into ½-inch slices

1 medium green chile, seeded and finely sliced

To serve

4 large portobello mushrooms

olive oil, for cooking and roasting

8 oz. cherry tomatoes on the vine

a few torn sage leaves

4 eggs

sea salt and freshly ground black pepper

a flat griddle pan or large skillet, preheated and lightly greased

4 oiled muffin rings, 3½-inches diameter

Serves 4

Makes 4 pancakes

Sift the flour, baking powder, and salt into a large bowl, then stir in the masa harina or cornmeal. Put the egg yolks into another bowl and beat in the buttermilk and milk. Add the flour mixture and beat to a thick batter. Stir in the Parmesan. Put the egg white into a clean bowl and beat until stiff peaks form, then fold into the batter with a metal spoon.

Meanwhile arrange the mushrooms in a roasting pan, stem side up. Sprinkle with olive oil, salt, and pepper and roast in a preheated oven at 400°F for 5 minutes. Add the tomatoes to the roasting pan, brush with a little extra olive oil, sprinkle with salt, pepper, and the torn sage leaves, then roast for a further 5 minutes.

Heat the prepared griddle or skillet over medium heat. Add the oiled muffin rings and heat well. Divide the bacon between the 4 muffin rings and sauté for 1 minute. Add a share of the scallions and chile, then add 2 tablespoons of the batter to each ring. When the mixture has risen and started to set, remove the rings. Turn the pancakes over and cook until brown. Transfer to a plate and keep them warm in a low oven while you cook the eggs.

Meanwhile, brush a large skillet with oil and heat well over high heat, then add the eggs and cook until the whites are set and the yolks still soft.

Put 1 pancake onto each plate. Add a mushroom, then put an egg on top. Finish the stack with a bunch of roasted tomatoes, then serve.

Belgian waffles are traditionally made in a deep, square waffle, iron which produces a thick waffle with deep wells to trap butter and syrup. The best use a yeast-raised batter, but don't let that put you off—it's definitely worth the effort. By doing the hard work the night before, all you need to do in the morning is add the eggs and bake.

Classic Belgian Waffles
with Strawberries and Praline Cream

Start the night before. Sift the flour, sugar, salt, and yeast into a large bowl. Stir in the cooled melted butter, milk, and vanilla extract to make a smooth mixture. Cover the bowl with plastic wrap and leave at room temperature overnight.

First thing in the morning, preheat the lightly greased waffle iron. Beat the egg yolks into the yeast mixture. Put the egg whites into a clean bowl and beat with a wire whisk until stiff peaks form. Carefully fold them into the batter with a metal spoon.

To make the praline cream, put the cream into a clean bowl and whip to a soft, loose consistency. Add the praline and stir it once or twice to give a marbled effect, then set aside and let the caramel bleed into the cream.

Before baking the waffles, assemble all the toppings and accompaniments—the best waffles are eaten the moment they're done.

Depending on the size of the waffle iron, pour about 1/2 cup of the batter into each heated compartment, close the lid (which will help spread out the batter), and cook until golden, about 3–5 minutes. Resist the temptation to open the lid for 3 minutes. There is nothing worse than an undercooked waffle: they should be crisp on the outside and served immediately. In a pinch, they can be kept warm in a low oven, but will lose some crispness. A quick reheating in the toaster works remarkably well.

Serve the waffles hot with a spoonful of praline cream and a few fresh strawberries.

2 cups all-purpose flour

2 tablespoons sugar

1 teaspoon salt

1 teaspoon active dry yeast

1½ sticks unsalted butter, melted and cooled

1½ cups milk

1 teaspoon vanilla extract

3 eggs, separated

8 oz. strawberries, to serve

Praline Cream

1¼ cups heavy cream

2 oz. hazelnut praline (page 60)

a deep Belgian waffle iron, preheated and lightly greased

Serves 4–6
Makes 12 waffles

wonderful waffles

Crisp Chocolate Waffles

As we all know, when it comes to chocolate, some people become quite irrational—chocolate is their passion. This recipe is for them. Always use the best quality chocolate you can find—remember the higher the cocoa solid content, the better the chocolate.

1½ cups all-purpose flour

2 tablespoons sugar

¼ cup unsweetened cocoa powder

1 teaspoon salt

1 package (¼ oz.) active dry yeast

7 tablespoons unsalted butter

6 oz. bittersweet chocolate, chopped

1½ cups milk

1 teaspoon vanilla extract

3 eggs, separated

To serve
hot chocolate sauce (page 60)
ice cream

a waffle iron, preheated and lightly greased

Serves 4
Makes 8–10 waffles

Start the night before. Sift the flour, sugar, cocoa powder, salt, and yeast into a large bowl. Put the butter and 2 oz. of the chocolate into a large saucepan and melt over gentle heat. Stir in the milk and vanilla extract. Beat the flour mixture into the warm chocolate, then transfer to a large bowl and cover with plastic wrap. Set aside at room temperature overnight.

First thing in the morning, turn on the lightly greased waffle iron. Beat the egg yolks into the yeast mixture and stir in the remaining 4 oz. chopped chocolate. Put the egg whites into a clean bowl and beat with a wire whisk until stiff peaks form. Gently fold them into the batter with a metal spoon.

Depending on the size of the waffle iron, spoon about ½ cup of the batter into each heated compartment, close the lid (which will help spread out the batter), and cook until crisp, about 4 minutes.

Serve the waffles cut or torn in half to reveal the oozing melted chocolate. Add ice cream and smother with hot chocolate sauce.

You will probably find you have all the ingredients for a basic waffle mix in your kitchen already, So this is truly a speedy recipe. I find that a light oil spray is best for greasing the waffle iron.

Quick Vanilla Waffles

with Chile-steeped Raspberries

1½ cups all-purpose flour

2 teaspoons baking powder

½ teaspoon salt

1 tablespoon sugar

3 eggs, separated

1 cup milk

5 tablespoons unsalted butter, melted and cooled

2 teaspoons pure vanilla extract

To serve

confectioners' sugar, for dusting

vanilla ice cream

chile-steeped raspberries (page 63)

a waffle iron, preheated and lightly greased

Serves 6–8

Makes 24 heart-shaped sandwiches

Sift the flour, baking powder, salt, and sugar into a large bowl. Put the egg yolks, milk, cooled melted butter, and vanilla extract into another bowl and mix well. Add the flour mixture to the milk mixture and beat until just mixed—don't overbeat.

Put the egg whites into a clean bowl and beat with a wire whisk until stiff peaks form. Gently fold the egg whites into the waffle batter with a metal spoon. It's important not to overmix at this stage, so if there are a few lumps of egg white floating around, leave them—it doesn't matter.

Spoon the batter into the hot waffle iron, spread the mixture out to the edges, and close the lid. (Most waffle irons take about ½ cup batter.) Electric waffle irons usually have an indicator light which goes off when the waffle is ready: if not, cook until the waffle is crisp and golden, about 3–5 minutes.

Sift the confectioners' sugar over the waffles, top with ice cream and raspberries, and serve. Alternatively, if you have a heart-shaped waffle, break it into segments and sandwich the hearts together with ice cream. Top with the raspberries.

Spicy Nut Waffles with Ginger Pears

Not all yeast batters need to be left for hours—you can cheat and still get some great results. The secret is to make sure everything is warm before you start, right down to the flour and the bowl—use the microwave defrost setting to raise the mixture in half the time.

Put the flour into a large microwavable bowl and warm on 100 percent setting for 10 seconds: this will help the yeast grow and speed up the rising process.

Put the warm milk, vanilla, cooled melted butter, and egg yolks into another bowl and mix well. Add the yeast, salt, sugar, cinnamon, and walnuts to the bowl of warm flour. Transfer the flour mixture to the milk mixture and stir until smooth. Cover with plastic wrap and leave in a warm place for 45 minutes or until doubled in size.

Put the wine into a saucepan large enough to fit the pears. Add the sugar, ginger, and 1¼ cups water and bring slowly to a boil over medium heat. Peel the pears and add them to the pan. Reduce the heat and simmer for 25 minutes, gently turning the pears from time to time, to make sure they cook evenly. Using a slotted spoon, carefully remove the pears to a plate. Boil the ginger liquid for 10 minutes to reduce it to a thin syrup. Strain to remove the ginger, then return the pears and syrup to the pan and let steep until ready to serve.

To finish the waffle mixture, put the egg whites into a clean bowl and beat with a wire whisk until stiff peaks form. Fold through the batter with a metal spoon.

Depending on the size of the waffle iron, spoon about ½ cup of the batter into the preheated compartments and cook until golden, about 4–5 minutes. Serve each waffle soaked in ginger syrup, topped with a pear or pears, a share of the crystallized or glacéed ginger, and topped with a spoonful of yogurt or whipped cream.

1½ cups all-purpose flour

1¼ cups warm milk

1 teaspoon vanilla extract

1 stick unsalted butter, melted and cooled

2 eggs, separated

1 teaspoon active dry yeast

½ teaspoon salt

2 tablespoons sugar

2 teaspoons ground cinnamon

8 oz. walnuts, finely chopped

Ginger pears

½ bottle sweet wine (375 ml) such as orange muscat or sauterne

3 mini pears or 1 large pear per person

⅔ cup sugar

2-inch piece of fresh ginger, peeled and finely sliced

To serve

5 oz. crystallized or glacéed ginger, finely sliced

yogurt or whipped cream

a waffle iron, preheated and lightly greased

Serves 4–6
Makes 6–8 waffles

This recipe makes a delicate waffle, jam-packed with fruit.
As the batter cooks, the raspberries soften and the juice seeps
into the fabric of the waffle giving a beautiful mottled effect.

Raspberry Waffles

with Pistachio and Peach Honey

1½ cups all-purpose flour

2 teaspoons baking powder

½ teaspoon salt

3 tablespoons sugar

3 eggs, separated

1 cup milk

4 tablespoons unsalted butter, melted and cooled

2 teaspoons vanilla extract

6 oz. fresh raspberries

To serve

sour cream or crème fraîche

peach and pistachio honey (page 63)

a waffle iron, preheated and lightly greased

Serves 4
Makes 8 waffles

Sift the flour, baking powder, salt, and sugar into a large bowl. Put the egg yolks, milk, cooled melted butter, and vanilla into another bowl and beat well. Briefly stir in the flour mixture until almost mixed.

Add the raspberries, crushing some with a spoon to give a marbled effect.

Put the egg whites into a clean bowl and beat with a wire whisk until stiff peaks form. Gently fold into the batter with a large metal spoon.

Depending on the size of the waffle iron, spoon about ¼–½ cup of the batter into the preheated compartments and cook until crisp, about 4–5 minutes.

Serve with sour cream and peach and pistachio honey.

Spiced Pumpkin Waffles

1½ cups all-purpose flour

3 teaspoons baking powder

½ teaspoon baking soda

1 teaspoon ground cinnamon

1 teaspoon freshly grated nutmeg

1 teaspoon ground ginger

a pinch of salt

½ teaspoon freshly ground
black pepper

2 eggs

¼ cup firmly packed brown sugar

8 oz. roasted pumpkin flesh,
fresh or canned (see recipe
introduction)

1⅔ cups milk

4 tablespoons unsalted butter,
melted and cooled

freshly grated zest of 1 orange

2 oz. pumpkin seeds (optional)

To serve

honey butter (page 60)

whipped cream (optional)

*a waffle iron, preheated and
lightly greased*

Serves 3–4
Makes 6–8 waffles

I first discovered these on Hallowe'en in San Francisco a few years ago. They are packed with spices and I think are best served simply with cool whipped cream and sugar. If the thought of attacking a pumpkin and cooking it fills you with apathy, you can use canned or, better still, use raw grated butternut squash or pumpkin. If you do, put it into a clean cloth and squeeze out the excess liquid (so the waffles won't be limp).

Sift the flour, baking powder, baking soda, cinnamon, nutmeg, ginger, salt, and pepper into a large bowl. Put the eggs, sugar, pumpkin, milk, cooled melted butter, and orange zest into a second bowl and beat well. Gently fold in the flour mixture.

Depending on the size of the waffle iron, spoon about ¼–½ cup of the batter into the preheated compartments and sprinkle with a few pumpkin seeds, if using. Cook until crisp, about 4–5 minutes. To achieve a frilly effect at the edges, as shown, use a little less mixture in the waffle iron.

Smother in honey butter, and serve with whipped cream, if using.

I love my pizzelle machine. It makes crisp wafers that can be molded into cones for ice cream. They also make quick cannoli shells. Cannoli are a favorite Italian treat enjoyed all over the world, consisting of fried pastry tubes stuffed with sweet ricotta and chocolate chips. Making the shells is beyond most home cooks, but, while not traditional, these "faux" cannoli are delicious and very pretty.

2 eggs

½ cup sugar

5 tablespoons unsalted butter, melted and cooled

1 teaspoon finely grated orange zest

1 teaspoon vanilla extract

2 cups all-purpose flour

½ teaspoon ground cinnamon

1 teaspoon baking powder

Cannoli filling

1 lb. fresh ricotta cheese

1¼ cups heavy cream

½ cup confectioners' sugar, sifted

1 teaspoon almond extract

1 teaspoon ground cinnamon

8 oz. bittersweet chocolate, grated

4 oz. shelled, unsalted pistachios, finely chopped

an electric pizzelle maker, preheated and lightly greased

a pastry bag fitted with a large plain tip

Makes 20

Pizzelle Cannoli

Put the eggs and sugar into a bowl and, using electric beaters, beat until pale. Add the cooled butter, orange zest, and vanilla. Sift in the flour, cinnamon, and baking powder, then, using a wooden spoon, beat well to form a dough.

Flour your hands, then pinch off small, walnut-size balls of dough. Squash each ball between your palms to form a disk. Put 1 disk in each heated compartment of the machine, then press the lid down and clip closed to spread the mixture into wafer-like cookies. Cook for 1–3 minutes, depending on the machine.

Remove the hot wafers and immediately wrap each one around a clean saucepan handle or the handle of a wooden spoon to make an open-ended tube. (As the wafer cools it will become brittle, so it is important to act swiftly.) Let cool completely, then use immediately or store in an airtight container for up to 1 month.

To make the filling, use the back of a wooden spoon to push the ricotta through a mesh into a bowl. Add the cream, confectioners' sugar, almond extract, and cinnamon, and beat until thick and creamy. (The mixture will remain fairly grainy so don't be alarmed.) Stir in half the grated chocolate (4 oz.) and transfer the filling to a pastry bag fitted with a large plain nozzle. Pipe the filling into both ends of the cannoli and make sure the whole tube is filled. Dip the ends in chopped pistachios or the remaining grated chocolate, then serve.

Buttermilk Waffles with Baked Amaretti Apricots

Buttermilk gives a wonderful tangy richness to this waffle, while cornmeal provides extra bite. Fabulous served sweet or savory. (Don't be tempted to undercook them—they benefit from a little extra time in the waffle iron.)

1½ cups all-purpose flour

2 teaspoons baking powder

1 teaspoon baking soda

½ teaspoon salt

2 tablespoons vanilla sugar (page 61) or sugar

½ cup instant polenta or fine cornmeal

1⅔ cups buttermilk

2½ tablespoons unsalted butter, melted and cooled

3 eggs, separated

Baked amaretti apricots

6 large apricots, halved

4 oz. blackberries or blueberries

8 oz. mascarpone cheese

4 amaretti cookies, crushed

¼ cup maple syrup

To serve

confectioners' sugar, sifted

maple syrup

a baking tray

a waffle iron, lightly greased and preheated

Serves 4–8
Makes 8 large waffles

To prepare the apricots, put them onto a baking tray, cut side up. Put the blackberries, mascarpone, crushed amaretti cookies, and maple syrup into a bowl and mix well. Spoon the mixture onto the apricots and bake in a preheated oven at 425°F for 10 minutes.

To make the waffles, sift the flour, baking powder, baking soda, salt, and sugar into a large bowl and stir in the polenta. Put the buttermilk, cooled melted butter, and egg yolks into another large bowl and beat well. Stir the flour mixture into the buttermilk mixture, then beat to form a smooth batter.

Put the egg whites into a clean bowl and beat with a wire whisk until stiff peaks form. Gently fold the egg whites into the waffle batter with a metal spoon, being careful not to overmix.

Depending on the size of the waffle iron, spoon ¼–½ cup of the batter into the preheated compartments, so it almost covers the base. Cook until golden, about 3–4 minutes.

Pile the waffles onto warmed plates, add the baked apricots, and sprinkle with confectioners' sugar. Serve with extra maple syrup on the side.

To make the sugar plums, put the quartered plums and spiced brown sugar into a bowl and toss to coat. Melt the butter in a small skillet over medium heat until it foams, then add all the plum pieces and gently sauté until caramelized. Add the lemon juice to loosen the butter syrup and set aside to keep warm while you prepare the waffles.

To make the waffles, put the all-purpose and whole-wheat flours into a large bowl, add the baking powder, salt, sugar, allspice, and pecans, and stir well.

Put the egg yolks into another bowl, add the milk, molasses, and cooled melted butter, and beat well. Add the flour mixture, stir well, then stir in the chopped apple. Put the egg whites into a clean bowl and beat with a wire whisk until stiff peaks form, then fold gently into the waffle batter with a metal spoon.

Depending on the size of the waffle iron, spoon about ½ cup of the batter into the preheated compartments, making sure each batch has lots of apple in it. Cook until crisp, about 3–5 minutes.

Serve the waffles immediately topped with warm plums and plenty of sticky plum juice.

1½ cups all-purpose flour

½ cup whole-wheat flour

2 teaspoons baking powder

½ teaspoon salt

2 tablespoons firmly packed brown sugar

1 teaspoon ground allspice

2 oz. pecans, chopped

2 eggs, separated

¾ cup milk

1 tablespoon molasses

4 tablespoons unsalted butter, melted and cooled

2 crisp apples, peeled, cored, and coarsely chopped

Sugar Plums

6 ripe plums, quartered and pitted

4 oz. spiced brown sugar (page 61)

2 tablespoons unsalted butter

freshly squeezed juice of ½ lemon

a waffle iron, lightly greased and preheated

Serves 4–6
Makes 8 waffles (deep Belgian size)

Apple Wholewheat Waffles with Sugar Plums

I always associate this recipe with fall, when all kinds of orchard fruits are in season. Allspice is the secret ingredient—it brings all the fruit and nut flavors together, and grinding your own allspice berries will make sure you get the full force of the spice. I keep a special pepper grinder just for allspice.

Cooking bacon in a waffle iron is no new thing, in fact it's very logical when you think about it. Not only does it let the smokiness of the prosciutto penetrate the waffle, but saves on washing up skillets too! Use thinly sliced prosciutto so it will cook right through.

Smoky Prosciutto Waffles

with Blackberry Maple Pour

1²/₃ cups all-purpose flour

2 teaspoons baking powder

1 teaspoon baking soda

½ teaspoon salt

1 tablespoon sugar

½ teaspoon dry mustard powder

2 oz. Parmesan cheese, grated

2 oz. ground semolina

3 eggs, separated

1 cup buttermilk

¼ cup olive oil

16 slices finely sliced smoked prosciutto or bacon

maple and blackberry pour (page 62), to serve

a waffle iron, lightly greased and preheated

Serves 4
Makes 8 waffles

Sift the flour, baking powder, baking soda, salt, sugar, and mustard into a large bowl, then stir in the grated Parmesan and semolina.

Put the egg yolks, buttermilk, and olive oil into another bowl and beat well. Add the flour mixture and mix well.

Put the egg whites into a clean bowl and beat with a wire whisk until stiff peaks form, then fold into the mixture with a metal spoon.

Depending on the size of the waffle iron, spoon about 3 tablespoons of the batter into each preheated compartment, so it almost covers the base. The batter should be quite thick, so spread it out with the back of a spoon, leaving enough room for it to spread and rise. Put 2 slices of the prosciutto on top of the batter, then carefully close the lid. Cook until crisp, about 4–5 minutes (the pancetta should be sizzling crisp around the edges).

Serve the waffles immediately with warm maple and blackberry pour.

Cheese on toast has always been a popular comfort food, so what better way start your weekend than with an oozing cheese waffle on which to build your favorite brunch. Most cheeses—from cottage cheese to Parmesan—will work, but for me a good strong Cheddar can't be beaten, especially with a touch of cayenne or dry mustard powder to spark up the flavor.

Morning-After Breakfast Waffles

¾ **cup plus 2 tablespoons all-purpose flour**

¾ **cup fine cornmeal**

2 teaspoons baking powder

½ **teaspoon salt**

2 eggs, separated

1 cup milk

¾ **cup sour cream or yogurt**

4 oz. Cheddar cheese, grated

2 tablespoons chopped fresh chives

To serve

4 bunches cherry tomatoes, on the vine

16 slices bacon

8 eggs

sea salt and freshly ground black pepper

olive oil, for cooking and roasting

a baking tray, greased

a waffle iron, preheated and lightly greased

Serves 4
Makes 8 waffles

Put the vines of tomatoes onto a greased baking tray, sprinkle with olive oil, season with salt and pepper, and roast in a preheated oven at 400°F for 5 minutes or until their skins blister.

To make the waffles, sift the flour, cornmeal, baking powder, and salt into a large bowl. Put the egg yolks into another bowl, add the milk, sour cream, and ¼ cup olive oil, and beat well. Add the flour mixture and beat well. Put the egg whites into a clean bowl and beat with a wire whisk until stiff peaks form. Using a large metal spoon, gently fold the egg whites, cheese, and chives into the waffle batter.

Brush a small skillet with olive oil, add the bacon, and sauté until crisp. Remove from the skillet and let drain on paper towels. Brush the skillet with oil again, add 4 slices of the cooked bacon, then break 2 eggs on top, and cook gently until done. Keep them warm.

Depending on the size of the waffle iron, spoon about ¼–½ cup of the batter into the preheated compartments. Cook until crisp, at least 4–5 minutes (cheese waffles taste so much better when well done). Transfer the hot waffle to a large plate, slide the bacon and eggs on top, and serve with the roasted tomatoes. Repeat to make the other servings.

Crêpes Suzette

This old favorite seems to have disappeared in recent years, but it's still up there with the greats.

To make the basic crêpes, put the flour into a food processor, add the salt, egg, egg yolk, milk and water mixture, and cooled melted butter and pulse for a few seconds until the batter is smooth. Chill for 30 minutes.

Heat the pan over medium heat, then lightly brush with butter, using paper towels to wipe away any excess. Spoon 2 tablespoons of the batter into the hot pan and quickly swirl it around to coat the base of the pan evenly but thinly. If you add too much batter just tip the extra back into the bowl and trim away the pouring trail. Cook the crêpe for 1 minute, then carefully turn it over and cook the other side. (Serve immediately with sugar and lemon, preserves, or chocolate, or use to make Crêpes Suzette or the Galette on the following page.)

To make the crêpe suzette sauce, put the butter, sugar, orange zest and juice, and Cointreau into a large skillet and gently warm through over low heat. When the sugar has dissolved, boil the mixture for 2 minutes to make a butter syrup.

Put the first crêpe into the skillet of hot orange butter and, using a spatula and fork, fold it into quarters and push it to the edge of the skillet to make room for the next one. Repeat until all the crêpes are coated in orange butter and folded in the skillet.

To finish, keep the skillet over a low flame and sprinkle the crêpes with the sugar, Cointreau, and rum. Quickly but very carefully, light the alcohol in the skillet with a match. Serve immediately before the flames disappear.

³/₄ cup all-purpose flour

½ teaspoon salt

1 egg

1 egg yolk

²/₃ cup milk mixed with
²/₃ cup water

3 tablespoons unsalted butter, melted and cooled

Crêpes suzette sauce

1 stick unsalted butter

¼ cup sugar

grated zest and juice of
2 oranges

3 tablespoons Cointreau, Grand Marnier, or apricot brandy

To finish

1 tablespoon sugar

2 tablespoons Cointreau, Grand Marnier, or apricot brandy

1 tablespoon dark rum

a crêpe pan, omelet pan, or small skillet, preheated to moderately hot, buttered

Serves 4
Makes 8–10 crêpes

Note *To store crêpes, stack them on a large plate until you need to reheat them. They can be kept warm by wrapping them in a dish towel and putting them on a plate set over a saucepan of simmering water.*

To freeze, stack with sheets of wax paper between, wrap in plastic wrap, then freeze.

crêpes, crumpets, and blini

1½ cups all-purpose flour

½ teaspoon salt

¼ cup sugar

4 eggs

2 cups plus 2 tablespoons milk

4 tablespoons unsalted butter, melted and cooled

2 tablespoons brandy

peanut oil, for brushing

Chocolate filling

4 egg yolks

½ cup sugar

2 teaspoons vanilla extract

1¼ cups heavy cream

8 oz. bittersweet chocolate, grated

7 oz. walnuts, finely chopped

To serve (optional)

1 cup heavy cream, lightly whipped

1 teaspoon ground cinnamon

finely grated zest of 1 orange

a crêpe pan or small skillet, 8 inches diameter

a springform cake pan, 8 inches diameter, buttered and bottom lined

buttered wax paper

Serves 8

Chocolate Galette

This is literally a pancake-cake, layered with sweet custard and chocolate and baked in the oven. A wedge of this curious striped chocolate dessert makes a great talking point.

To make the batter, put the flour into a food processor, add the salt, sugar, eggs, milk, cooled melted butter, and brandy, and pulse for a few seconds until smooth. Heat the crêpe pan, brush with peanut oil, then wipe away with excess with paper towels. Cook the crêpes as in the Basic Crêpe recipe on page 52. You should have at least 15, depending on how thin you make them.

To make the filling, put the egg yolks and sugar into a bowl and beat until pale and thick. Beat in the vanilla and cream.

Put a crêpe in the base of the prepared cake pan, spread it with a little vanilla cream mixture and sprinkle with grated chocolate and chopped walnuts. Repeat the layers until you run out of crêpes or fill the pan. Finish with a crêpe and cover the top with a piece of buttered wax paper.

Bake in a preheated oven at 350°F for 30 minutes. Remove from the oven and let cool slightly before unclipping the pan and transferring the galette to a serving plate.

Serve sliced into wedges, topped with lightly whipped cream flavored with cinnamon and orange zest, if using.

Good English crumpets remind me of my childhood, and this homemade version is even more wonderful than the store-bought kind. I like to use fresh yeast—available in small bakeries or sometimes from in-supermarket bakeries—but in case you can't find it, use active dry yeast instead.

Tea and Crumpets

1¼ cups milk mixed with 1¼ cups water

½ oz. compressed yeast*

3 cups all-purpose flour

½ teaspoon baking soda

1 teaspoon salt

To serve

unsalted butter

berry jam or honey

tea

2–3 crumpet rings or biscuit cutters

a flat griddle pan or skillet, preheated and greased

Makes 12

*To use active dry yeast, mix one ¼ oz. package with the flour

Warm the milk and water mixture in a small saucepan. If using fresh yeast, put it into a small bowl with a little of the warm liquid, stir well, then add the remaining milk and water. Sift the flour into a mixing bowl, then stir in the warm yeast mixture. (I find the easiest way to get a smooth batter is to use your hand.)

Cover the bowl with a clean cloth and leave in a warm place for 1 hour. Put the baking soda and salt into a bowl, add 2 tablespoons water, mix well, then beat it into the mixture. Set aside for a further 45 minutes.

Put the greased crumpet rings on the prepared griddle pan and set over medium heat. When the rings are hot, spoon 2 tablespoons of the batter into each ring—just enough to cover the base. Let cook for about 4–5 minutes, until the underside is golden, then remove the rings and turn the crumpet over to brown the top.

To serve, toast the crumpets on both sides, smother them with butter, and stack on a hot plate. Serve with extra butter and a dish of berry jam or honey. A cup of tea is the traditional accompaniment.

2/3 cup all-purpose flour

2/3 cup buckwheat flour

1/2 teaspoon salt

1/2 teaspoon active dry yeast

1 tablespoon sugar

1 1/4 cups warm milk

2 tablespoons heavy cream, lightly whipped

1 egg, separated

sour cream, to serve

Dill pickled salmon

10 oz. thick-cut smoked salmon

1 tablespoon chopped dill

1 small cucumber, about 6 inches, chopped

2 tablespoons grated raw beet

Dressing

freshly squeezed juice of 2 limes

2 teaspoons sugar

1 mild red chile, seeded and finely chopped

sea salt and freshly ground black pepper

4 blini pans or a skillet, lightly greased

Serves 4
Makes 4 blini

The blin (plural blini) is probably the most famous food ever to come out of Russia. They are cooked in a small iron frying pan, called a blini pan, like the one in the picture. However, you don't need a special pan—blini cooked in a regular large skillet or on a flat griddle taste just as authentic, even if they look a bit freeform. Smoked salmon, sour cream, and caviar is another traditional topping.

Buckwheat Blini

Sift the flour and buckwheat flour into a large bowl, add the salt, yeast, and sugar. Make a hollow in the center and add the warm milk, and egg yolk. Gradually mix into a smooth batter, cover with plastic wrap, and set aside in a warm place for 1 hour.

Beat the egg white until stiff peaks form and fold it through the risen batter with a metal spoon. Fold in the whipped cream. Heat the prepared blini pan(s) over medium heat and spoon in enough mixture to cover the base of the pan. If making in a skillet, each blin should be about 4 inches diameter. Turn it over when bubbles rise to the surface and the base is lightly browned.

To make the dill pickled salmon, cut the salmon into 1/4-inch pieces and put into a medium bowl. Add the dill, cucumber, and beets. To make the dressing, put the lime juice, sugar, and chile into a separate bowl and beat with a fork. Add the dressing to the salmon, toss gently, then add salt and pepper to taste.

Serve the warm blini with sour cream and a spoonful of the dill pickled salmon.

sauces and toppings

Honey Butter

1½ sticks unsalted butter, softened

grated zest of 1 lemon

⅓ cup thick honey

Makes 10 oz.

Put the butter and lemon zest into a food processor and process until smooth. With the motor running, add the honey and blend until pale. Transfer to a lidded container and store for up to 2 weeks in the refrigerator (it will set as it chills).

Hot or Cold Chocolate Sauce

1¼ cups heavy cream

1 tablespoon brandy

8 oz. bittersweet chocolate, broken

1 tablespoon light corn syrup

3 tablespoons unsalted butter

Serves 4–6: Makes 2 cups

Put the cream and brandy into a saucepan and heat until almost boiling. Add the chocolate, corn syrup, and butter and stir until the the chocolate has melted and the sauce is smooth. Serve hot or cold.

Cinnabutter

2½ sticks unsalted butter, softened

2 tablespoons milk

¾ cup confectioners' sugar

4 teaspoons ground cinnamon

1 teaspoon freshly grated nutmeg

Makes 10 oz.

Put all the ingredients into a small bowl and beat with electric beaters until pale and creamy. Transfer to a lidded container and store in the refrigerator. Alternatively, spoon it onto a piece of plastic wrap, roll it into a log, and chill (cut a slice when you need it). Keeps for 2 weeks in the refrigerator.

Hazelnut Praline

4 oz. hazelnuts, about ¾ cup

½ cup sugar

Makes 8 oz.

Lightly oil a baking tray. Put the nuts and sugar into a saucepan over low heat until the sugar melts. As it begins to brown, stir briefly with a metal spoon and continue cooking until the sugar is a good caramel color. Pour the mixture onto the oiled baking tray and let cool.

Break up the cold praline with a rolling pin, put the pieces into a plastic bag, wrap it in a dish towel, and tap with the pin to form a coarse powder. Store in an airtight container.

Vanilla Sugar

3 cups sugar
6 vanilla beans
Makes 3 cups

Put the sugar into a food processor. Split the vanilla beans lengthwise leaving them attached at one end. Using a sharp knife, scrape the seeds out of the beans and into the sugar. Set aside the beans. Blend briefly to distribute the vanilla seeds, then pack the sugar and the spent bean into a large glass bottle. The longer you leave it, the stronger the flavor. It lasts for months, so make a large batch.

Spiced Brown Sugar

3 cups firmly packed brown sugar
2 cinnamon sticks, broken,
plus 2 whole sticks, to store
1 teaspoon allspice berries
1 teaspoon whole cloves
finely grated zest of 1 lemon
Makes about 1½ lb.

Put the sugar into a food processor, add the broken cinnamon sticks, allspice, cloves, and lemon zest, and grind to a coarse powder. Sift through a wide-meshed sieve and discard any large pieces of spice. Store the spiced sugar in an airtight container with 2 cinnamon sticks.

Toffee Sauce

7 tablespoons unsalted butter
⅓ cup firmly packed brown sugar
4 oz. light corn syrup
¼ cup heavy cream
Makes about 1½ cups

Put all the ingredients into a saucepan and heat gently, stirring constantly, until the sugar has dissolved. Boil for 3 minutes, then serve immediately or let cool and store in an airtight container in the refrigerator for up to 1 week.

Orange and Cardamom Syrup

2 cups sugar

1¾ cups orange juice, strained

8 cardamom pods, bruised

finely peeled zest of 1 orange

Makes 2¾ cups

Put all the ingredients into a saucepan and heat gently over low heat until the sugar has dissolved. Increase the heat and boil the syrup for 10 minutes—or longer for a thicker consistency. Cool and store in the refrigerator for up to 2 weeks. Leave the zest and pods in the syrup to store it, but strain before using. (The syrup will thicken as it cools.)

Maple and Blackberry Pour

4 oz. blackberries

1 cup maple syrup

a piece of lemon zest

Makes 1½ cups

Put all the ingredients into a saucepan and heat gently over low heat until the syrup is almost boiling and the berries have begun to let out their juice. Let the syrup stand for 5 minutes to infuse and cool slightly, remove the lemon zest and serve.

Apple Marmalade

3 tablespoons unsalted butter

3 baking apples, peeled, cored, and sliced

grated zest of ½ lemon

½ cup firmly packed brown sugar

Makes 8 oz.

Melt the butter in a large saucepan over low heat and add the apples, lemon zest, and 2 tablespoons water. Cook the apples until soft and pulpy, then press them through a sieve into a bowl. Beat in the sugar, return the mixture to a clean pan, and boil until you have a thick purée. Cool slightly and serve or store in the refrigerator for up to 2 weeks.

Blueberry Sauce

1 tablespoon arrowroot

3 tablespoon vanilla sugar (page 60) or sugar

10 oz. blueberries

freshly squeezed juice of 1 lemon

Makes 2 cups

Put the arrowroot and 1 tablespoon water into a bowl and stir to make a thin paste. Transfer to a saucepan, add the sugar, blueberries, and 1¼ cups water, and bring to a boil, stirring constantly. Simmer for 10 minutes, remove from the heat and stir in the lemon juice. Serve hot or store in the refrigerator for up to 1 week.

Chile-steeped Raspberries

2 bird's eye chiles, seeded

6 oz. raspberries

2 tablespoons framboise or brandy

1 cup sugar

Makes 1½ cups

Put the chiles, raspberries, and framboise into a bowl. Put the sugar into a saucepan, add ¾ cup water and heat gently over low heat until the sugar has dissolved, then boil for 5 minutes until thickened and reduced. Pour the hot syrup over the raspberries, stir once, then cover and leave for at least 2 hours to develop the flavors. Remove the chiles before serving.

Mango and Ginger Purée

2 ripe mangoes, peeled and chopped

1 inch fresh ginger, peeled and grated

freshly squeezed juice of 1 lime

2 tablespoons confectioners' sugar

Makes 1¾ cups

Put the mango into a blender. Squeeze the grated ginger to extract the juice. Add the juice to the mango and discard the gratings. Blend well, add the lime juice, sugar, and a little water if necessary. Strain the sauce and serve immediately, or store in the refrigerator for up to 2 days.

Peach and Pistachio Honey

2 firm peaches, skinned and pitted

1½ cups clear orange blossom honey

1 tablespoon peach schnapps (optional)

2 oz. shelled unsalted pistachios*

Makes 2 cups

*Pistachios from a Middle Eastern store will be very bright green.

Cut the peach flesh into ⅛-inch cubes. Put the honey and schnapps, if using, into a saucepan and heat until almost boiling. Add the chopped peaches and pistachios and let cool slightly. Serve warm as a spooning sauce.

index

conversion charts

Weights and measures have been rounded up or down slightly to make measuring easier.

volume equivalents

American	Metric	Imperial
1 teaspoon	5 ml	
1 tablespoon	15 ml	
¼ cup	60 ml	2 fl. oz.
⅓ cup	75 ml	2½ fl. oz.
½ cup	125 ml	4 fl. oz.
⅔ cup	150 ml	5 fl. oz. (¼ pint)
¾ cup	175 ml	6 fl. oz.
1 cup	250 ml	8 fl. oz.

weight equivalents

Imperial	Metric
1 oz.	25 g
2 oz.	50 g
3 oz.	75 g
4 oz.	125 g
5 oz.	150 g
6 oz.	175 g
7 oz.	200 g
8 oz. (½ lb.)	250 g
9 oz.	275 g
10 oz.	300 g
11 oz.	325 g
12 oz.	375 g
13 oz.	400 g
14 oz.	425 g
15 oz.	475 g
16 oz. (1 lb.)	500 g
2 lb.	1 kg

measurements

Inches	Cm
¼ inch	5 mm
½ inch	1 cm
¾ inch	1.5 cm
1 inch	2.5 cm
2 inches	5 cm
3 inches	7 cm
4 inches	10 cm
5 inches	12 cm
6 inches	15 cm
7 inches	18 cm
8 inches	20 cm
9 inches	23 cm
10 inches	25 cm
11 inches	28 cm
12 inches	30 cm

oven temperatures

110°C	(225°F)	Gas ¼
120°C	(250°F)	Gas ½
140°C	(275°F)	Gas 1
150°C	(300°F)	Gas 2
160°C	(325°F)	Gas 3
180°C	(350°F)	Gas 4
190°C	(375°F)	Gas 5
200°C	(400°F)	Gas 6
220°C	(425°F)	Gas 7
230°C	(450°F)	Gas 8
240°C	(475°F)	Gas 9